Marathon Running

From First Time to Faster Time

Marathon Running – From First Time to Faster Time

1. Acknowledgments — 5
2. Getting Started — 6
3. Common Terms — 8
4. Goals and Objectives — 10
5. Essential Kit — 12
    - Footwear — 12
    - Running Gear — 18
    - Timing Devices — 19
6. Training — 21
    - Training Basics — 22
    - Be Specific — 27
    - Programs — 28
    - Motivation — 28
    - Tapering — 32
    - Avoiding Injury — 33
    - Benchmarking — 35
7. Sample Training Programs — 37
8. Running Technique — 41
    - Strike! — 41
    - Cadence — 43
    - Breathing — 44
    - Posture and Position — 46
9. Nutrition — 48
    - Carbohydrate — 48
    - Fat — 54
    - Protein — 55
    - Other tips — 57

10. Race Day   58
    - Basics   58
    - Start Line   58
    - Pace   59
    - Fuelling   61
    - 3 Phases   63
11. Going Faster   68
    - Weights and Exercises   68
    - Body Mass   69
12. Summing Up   71
13. After the Event   73
    - Recovery   73
    - Maintenance   74
14. About the Author   76
15. Further Reading   79

1. Acknowledgments

For taking time to read and review, and for their invaluable feedback, I would like to thank the following people:

- For his constant enthusiasm for all things related to running, and involvement in of local and national events in Germany - Dirk Schulte-Eversum
- For his expert knowledge of the human anatomy, and for making me get up to run on Sunday mornings - Dr. Gary Minto
- As an inspiration to any runner at any level, and for his feedback on my guide, from one of the very best - Kerry Liam-Wilson
- And to Rachel Bunting and Gareth Noble, for their comments and notes

Most importantly, thanks to my wife Jo, for her patience and constant support of me in the sport I love; and my three brilliant girls - Jessica, Ava and Edie.

2. Getting started

If you have just signed up for your first marathon, then congratulations! You will join a small but growing group of people who want to complete a goal that many believe they could never achieve.

We are often discouraged by other people or more often by ourselves – that we are too slow, too unfit, not a runner and so on – but I strongly believe that almost everyone has the capability to complete a marathon. However, if you have not run seriously before, you should consider that the 18-week programs included are based only on your final training towards the marathon. You should start running as early as possible, even if you build up over 12 months, running short distances every 2 or 3 days. The longer you can spend building 'Muscle Memory', the more this will help you during the race.

For more experienced runners, in almost every case we have the ability to go faster. Normally we are limited by commitment, time, and motivation.

There is a huge range of practical advice available to modern runners, and you can find excellent training plans and advice online. I want to provide real-world tips and advice which will help runners to complete their first marathon, and also to help improving runners to hit their goals.

The advice contained is grouped in some cases for **first time** runners, or for repeat runners seeking a **faster time**, under relevant headings for each.

For further reading, particularly if you are intending to improve on previous marathon times, I would strongly recommend the excellent 'Advanced Marathoning' by Pete Pfitzinger. It is quite technical, but the advice is solid.

Also, for beginners and improving runners, I would recommend Hal Higdon (www.halhigdon.com). I used his advanced program as my first 'serious' training program, and he caters for all levels.

I have also included a short section on further reading at the end of the guide.

3. Common Terms

It is worth being familiar with some of the terms commonly used amongst runners:

- Cadence – the number of times your feet hit the floor, generally quoted per minute. A normal cadence is somewhere in the range 160-200 strikes per minute.
- Carb / Carbohydrate – one of the 2 energy sources used by the body, and used in a higher proportion than fat at higher intensities.
- CV (Cardiovascular) – heart and lung 'fitness', its ability to deliver oxygen to the muscles and dispel carbon dioxide, which is improved through training.
- Fade – an anticipated slow-down in the final miles, especially for first time marathon runners. Can be avoided with correct race strategy, pacing, and fuelling.
- Fartlek – Swedish for 'speed-play', this is a training technique which mixes short bursts of climbing, speed or lunging with regular running. Basically, just mixing it up.
- Fat – one of the 2 energy sources used by the body, and used in a higher proportion than carbohydrate at lower intensities
- Fuelling – taking on calories (through food, drink and gels) during the race or in training
- Hydration – taking on water during the race or in training
- Kinesiology Tape – used by runners to take pressure off the muscles, increase blood flow, and relieve pain.
- Lactate Threshold (Anaerobic Threshold) – this is the point above which lactic acid levels rise rapidly (due to a

rapid growth in the proportion of anaerobic carb-burning at higher intensities)
- Program – the training plan or schedule
- Pronation – the 'roll' of the foot during the strike and rebound phase of the cycle. Your natural pronation can be compensated through selection of training shoes.
- Protein – required by the body to rebuild the muscles after long distance or high intensity training.
- Split – can mean any mid-race measure of time, but also describes the race strategy for the marathon – negative split is faster on the second half, neutral is equal times for first half and second half, and positive split is slower on the second half (ie. with an anticipated 'fade').
- Stride – the length of your stride between foot-strikes, which when combined with cadence gives your speed. Higher cadence, and higher stride length lead to greater speed.
- Strike – how the foot hits the ground, normally described as forefoot (landing on the balls of your feet), midfoot (where the foot lands flat), and heel-strike (where the heel contacts the ground first).
- Taper – the period immediately prior to the race, normally 2-3 weeks, where you should reduce your training intensity to rest the body in preparation for the race.

4. Goals and Objectives

First time

Before you start your training program, just take a moment to remind yourself why you have decided to do this. Is it for charity, personal achievement, feeling fitter, 'bucket-list' goal? Whatever the reason, write it down or say it to yourself, and on the days when the training is hard-going, you can call this up. You will need it during your training program.

Visualising can really help. This doesn't necessarily mean visualising crossing the line at 26.2 miles. Generally, the trick is to visualise the steps that are required to achieve your goal, and commit to them. So, you should keep in mind the image of breaking the tape – but it is equally or more important to visualise your training diary, the daily routine, the routes themselves and the other small sacrifices that you will have to make over the coming weeks - then commit to making them. It can also help to share your goal with your partner, friends, other runners, or in public. If it seems like a huge commitment, remember it's only for a few weeks….

However, you should ask yourself the following questions:

- How will I find the time for the training? Have I planned when this will be done?
- Is my partner ready for the odd times when I might be unavailable? For me, I found a good method was to set off on an early run to arrive back before the kids got up, or to set off to a rendezvous point with the family at the beach, swimming pool, brunch with friends etc, where you can shower and change and then carry on with your day.

- What are the costs involved? Running is very cheap, and you don't need to spend lots of money on kit. However, entry and travel costs for bigger marathons can be expensive, and a local event can be very cost effective by comparison, and often equally enjoyable.
- Have I left myself enough time to prepare?
- Have I had a recent check-up with a doctor, just to make sure I'm in good health?

Faster time

You must accept that whilst you might not necessarily have to purely increase your training hours, realistically you will have to increase the intensity of your previous training program. This generally requires that you increase distance, increase speed, and introduce a proportion of training at an 'uncomfortable' level (basically pushing yourself at intensities that will hurt)

Vary your runs, push your limits, and factor in additional time for training that extends beyond purely running (weights and strength exercises, calisthenics, stretches and yoga).

Prepare for this additional effort, and commit to your program.

5. Essential Kit

Footwear

First time

- Seek advice – it is worth speaking to running specialist. People run in different styles, and whilst a new pair of shoes won't turn you into Emil Zatopek overnight, some basic advice will help you avoid a lot of unnecessary pain and discomfort. If you are running without pain, then you will be less likely to skip sessions, and ultimately this will have a significant effect on your training program, and therefore your fitness. So, *shoes are very important.*

- Cushioning – don't be tempted by lightweight, low-cushioned shoes. For marathon runners, cushioning is very important, and as a first-time marathoner you will not have the strength to allow you to run in lightweight shoes without injury. The advantage with low-cushioned shoes is weight, and arguably a change in style that can lead to more efficiency, however I would not advise this without plenty of experience. In my view, a cushioned shoe is the best option for general training. For first timers, I would recommend a pair for training, and a pair for racing. Modern running shoes can be fairly lightweight and cushioned, and if this is your first time, worry about comfort first and foremost. Aim for a cushioned shoe around the 250-300g mark for training, and the same or slightly lighter (around 200g) for race day (NB. 'race day' shoe is not only to be used during the race – you should have broken the shoe in during training, for at least 60 miles total, and one long run over 12 miles).

- Ankles – some prefer that the heel is 'locked' into place with a firm 'cup' at the back of the shoe. My personal view is that the heel should be supported, but allowed some movement within the shoe, as this helps to increase strength in the foot rather than relying on the shoe. If you are unsure seek advice from a dedicated running shop.

- Pronation – this is the degree of 'roll outwards' or 'roll inwards' that is natural to your foot strike. If you have an exaggerated style either way, you can select shoes which counter this. Pronation is common in most runners, to a greater or lesser extent, and shoes that account for this can help you to avoid injury.

- Toe box and sizing – should be wide enough for you to spread your toes a little, and have a small gap at the front. Otherwise the result will be discomfort, bruising to the toe nails, and possible loss of nails. Play around with the tightness of lacing, to find a good compromise which holds the foot firmly across the bridge, without causing pain.

- Consider going up one half-size compared to your normal size, as you will likely expand into this extra space during long runs (and buy your shoes in the afternoon, when your feet will be a little larger than the morning).

- Arches and insteps – feet differ greatly, so make sure that your arch is well-supported, and your instep is not being compressed when your shoes are firmly tied.

- Pick a specialist running brand. There are countless manufacturers competing for your attention, but you might look for the brands that specialise in running. Talk to other runners and take advice, as shoes are critical – Saucony, ASICS, Mizuno, Adidas, Brooks, and Salomon are very common, and although not a running-specific brand, I am a big fan of New Balance.

- Manufacturers will tend to recommend that you should change your shoes frequently. I would suggest that you can run in a good pair of shoes for 400-500 miles (and hence have more shoes!), provided that you are not heavy, hard-hitting, heel-striking, and running on hard surfaces. If you are, consider that you should have a shoe with heavier cushioning. There will be a noticeable 'flatness', or lack of rebound in the shoe, once they are due for a change. During an 18 week training program, you should therefore expect to have a couple of pairs, plus your race day shoes. Ultimately, it is hard to judge this, so keep in mind that shoes will degrade more quickly on hard surfaces, and try to avoid putting them through the washing machine or dryer. If you do, make this a cold wash cycle.

- As a first-timer, you should probably be running a maximum of 40 miles per week, over 14-18 weeks, so a couple of pairs of training shoes should be sufficient, and also gives you a dry pair of shoes if you have been running in the rain the previous day. In addition, I like to have a pair of race day shoes, as these are somehow 'special'. *The main thing is that you should have run at least 60 miles in your race day shoes, including 1-2 'long runs' of 13 miles or more.*

- If you have different brands of shoes, this can be an advantage, as the design of different shoes will strengthen your feet in different ways.

Above all, be prepared to spend some time finding what is right for you, and be brutal if the shoe does not fit! I wish I had realised 2 months earlier, before I lost 2 toe nails and lost all feeling in my middle toe, that I was running a half-size too small in my favourite brand. With the same shoe, only one half-size bigger, I ran high mileage with no pain, and no problems.

Also, you should be aiming to run in shoes that are around £80-£120 at retail price. However, you can often buy the previous season's model, often in unpopular colours, which can reduce the cost by up to 70%.

Faster Time

As a previous marathon runner, you will already know what you like and don't like in a shoe. However, you can achieve weight saving with your choice of shoe. Essentially, this is a shoe with less cushioning. The downside of this is that a less-cushioned race shoe will be harder on your body, particularly if you heel-strike. Also, a less cushioned shoe will extend the Achilles more than a shoe with a higher, cushioned heel. This can create a risk of damage during training, or worse than this during the race.

So what is the answer? I spent 2 years playing around with different shoes, ending up with a lot of shoes in the garage. I settled on the three types broadly described below:

1. Training Shoe (right, below) – 250g-325g (approx. 24-30mm heel, 8-12mm drop, well-cushioned)
2. Transition Shoe (centre, below)– 200g-250g (approx. 20-24mm heel, 4-8mm drop, moderately-cushioned)
3. Race Day Shoe (left, below) – less than 200g (approx. 16-20mm heel, 0-4mm drop, minimal cushioning)
    - NB. this last option is not suitable for you if you are a novice, a hard-hitting runner, or heavy. In this case, stay with options 1 and 2 for your race.

The 'training shoe' is comfortable, good for medium and long runs, and even for sessions on firmer ground. But if you want to run a lighter shoe on race day, you must build strength in the arches, forefoot and calf, and get the Achilles tendon used to increased extension. It can be hard to move to a 'racing flat' without causing injury, so the 'transition' shoe can help you to move from a more cushioned shoe to a lighter racing shoe without damage. I only ran in this 'transition' shoe for a maximum of 13 miles, building up from 3 miles over a period of 6 months. So bear in mind, you might already be too late this season to make any significant changes to your type of running and racing shoe. Be **very** patient, and make gradual changes. I would suggest very small runs initially, no more than one mile.

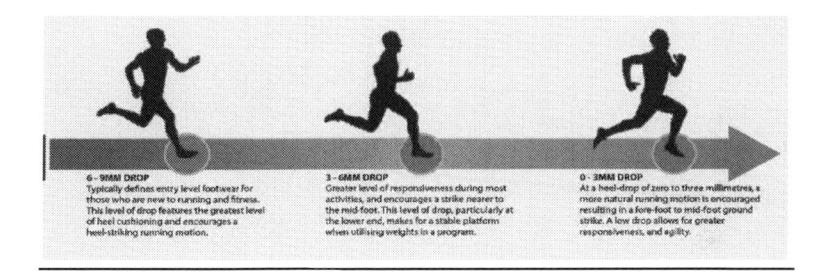

6 - 9MM DROP
Typically defines entry level footwear for those who are new to running and fitness. This level of drop features the greatest level of heel cushioning and encourages a heel-striking running motion.

3 - 6MM DROP
Greater level of responsiveness during most activities, and encourages a strike nearer to the mid-foot. This level of drop, particularly at the lower end, makes for a stable platform when utilising weights in a program.

0 - 3MM DROP
At a heel-drop of zero to three millimetres, a more natural running motion is encouraged resulting in a fore-foot to mid-foot ground strike. A low drop allows for greater responsiveness, and agility.

Running gear

First time

Training - a degree of common sense is required, but you don't need to spend a fortune. Make sure you have layers, so that you can remove or add as required. A lightweight waterproof is pretty much an essential in Northern Europe, as are leggings from November through February. I generally wear a short-sleeve running shirt and shorts during the summer, adding a lightweight fleece, waterproof jacket and hat for the autumn and winter. These can be removed during a session, and stuffed in a pocket, or tied around your waist.

This is the 'Onion Strategy', where you can peel off layers as you heat up. Don't forget that you cannot tie short-sleeve shirts around you, so a sensible strategy for a cool day would be a running shirt / vest, then a long sleeve fleece or second layer, then a waterproof jacket.

Remember to cover your head in the winter, as most heat is lost here, and to cover with a light cap or bandana during the summer to protect from the sun.

Race day – this is much more important. Top half - lightweight running vest, or running shirt (breathable, not cotton); bottom half – running shorts, or Lycra shorts. As you run, you will sweat, so heavier materials will become heavy and will chafe during a race. As with any good vehicle, you need to grease the moving parts…..make sure that you heavily lubricate (Vaseline is best) the areas around the thighs, groin, bum, armpits, nipples, and toes.

Faster Time

Race day - you need to concentrate on minimising the weight and drag in all areas, so dedicated running shorts and vest, or fitted Lycra clothing is essential. I prefer running shorts and vest, after some experimenting – they just feel more comfortable. If you are able to reduce the weight of your race-day running shoes without causing injury (see Running Technique), then this can greatly help.

Timing devices

These are a great tool for tracking your pace, and a great motivator if you are measuring performance against previous runs. It will help you significantly during training, and I would highly recommend that you use one. Basic models can be bought for less the £100. However, as you increase your running frequency, you will learn to recognise a particular pace +/- 10-15 seconds per mile. Also, GPS devices are sometimes a little inaccurate over short distances and off-road routes. Hence, if you also have some measured-distance segments, these can be really helpful. The most important thing is to follow the training program you have set, at the determined degrees of effort (EASY, MEDIUM or INTERVALS - HARD). I would recommend having some routes of known-mileage, but you should use the GPS watch for the lactate (pace) run and long run, so that you are familiar with this on the race day.

For speedwork (intervals), if you can find a running track, this is ideal. Otherwise, use your GPS watch or bicycle to map out sections of 400m, 800m and 1600m – then use a basic stopwatch function without GPS.

It's better to focus on covering the time or distance at the required level of effort for that session, and improving your form, rather than being slavish about the GPS.

My favourite regular run is an out-and-back riverside run, 7 miles total. I have recorded the mile points along the run, and hence can measure my pace easily without a GPS watch, and add in a fast mile during the mid-phase or at the finish.

It can also help to use the heart rate monitor, firstly to assess whether you are working too hard on longer runs, and to track your recovery time after sessions. A good recovery will see you return to below 130 bpm in 2 minutes, and this is a nice motivator as you become fitter. Also, your resting pulse can be a good indicator of whether you are overtraining, but this might be a little complex for this guide. If you feel very tired, or overworked, then go easy or skip a day.

6. Training

In general, your training schedule (afterwards referred to as your 'program'), should be between 14 and 18 weeks, depending on your existing level of experience and fitness, and your goals. But note this is just the time when you are seriously following a program, and you should ideally be building up 2-3 months, before you start the program.

Normally, it is necessary to book a long time in advance, so you will normally know you have a place at least 6 months ahead of the race. Use this time….

Pick your race to suit your ideal training, if this is possible. For example, I prefer to train outside in the early mornings, so I aim for late season (September / October) races. This way, I can build up through the spring and summer, peaking at the end of August, or early September. If you select an early season marathon (in the northern hemisphere), then most of your morning or evening training will be in darkness or at the gym during the week, so longer runs would be at the weekend.

Training basics

<u>Pace</u>

Firstly, you should set a realistic time goal for the race, as all the training sessions follow from this. Approximate per mile times are listed below, for different finish times:

- 3 hour marathon   6:52 per mile
- 4 hour marathon   9:10 per mile
- 5 hour marathon   11:27 per mile
- 6 hour marathon   13:44 per mile.

I would suggest going for a short run, of 2 or 3 miles, at a comfortable pace. Compare this pace to the above, and bear in mind that you will significantly improve over the training program, and then set a goal. If you have run 10k or half marathons before, this is a great help. As a rough guide:

Marathon pace = 10k time x 5 - 5½

Marathon pace = (½ marathon time x 2) plus 15-20 minutes

However, runners vary greatly from those who have great endurance, but are not fast over 10k, and vice versa. This is down to the natural make up of muscle, VO2 capacity, and many other factors. So you should work out if you are naturally fast, but looking to build stamina; or alternatively if you have good endurance, but want or need to increase your speed. Then you can modify your training program accordingly with higher mileage, or more speedwork.

Program Basics

There are three keystone runs that make up a good training program, as a beginner or an improving runner. If you are only able to train three times per week, then these are the runs you should complete.

- **Long run** – this increases stamina, and builds up strength in key muscle groups that you will need during the race. It also provides an essential psychological boost, as you build up to around 20 miles towards the end of the training program and realise that your goal is well within reach. Generally this should be run at a pace 1-2 minutes slower than your intended race pace. So for a 4 hour marathon, you would complete your slow runs at a pace of around 10:30 per mile. For beginners, you should not run over 3 hours in any one session.

- **Lactate Threshold (LT) / Anaerobic Threshold run** – the Lactate Threshold is the point at which the body starts to burn a high proportion of carbohydrate in preference to fat. This is quite hard to measure, so consider that this is a run that is uncomfortably hard, such that you cannot maintain a sustained conversation. You should be at around 80-85% of maximum effort. There is much evidence that running at this threshold will over time increase your ability to burn fat in preference to carbohydrate. This is important for maintaining your reserves of energy during the race, as you will be able to run at a higher intensity without burning up supplies of carbohydrate. The body can only store a limited amount of carbohydrate, and compared to fat it is an inefficient form of energy production. However, fat burning requires ample supplies of oxygen, hence at higher intensities the oxygen supply cannot be maintained for fat burning and the body draws on carb reserves. *If you can raise the threshold (ie. the intensity level at which your body suddenly shifts to a rapidly growing proportion of carbohydrate burning), then you can run faster for longer without running out of fuel.*

- **Speedwork session** – for first time runners, you might consider replacing this with a medium pace run, containing short bursts of speed, lunges (long strides), or pushing the pace up a climb. For more experienced marathon runners looking to improve, ***I believe this makes the biggest difference to your potential finish time.*** The session is made up of a number of short runs (400m, 800m, 1-mile or 2-mile), completed at a pace that is around 30 seconds to 60 seconds faster than your intended race pace.

Both the Lactate (Pace) Run and Speedwork will increase the ability of the body to break down the by-products of carbohydrate metabolisis (known as lactates). These build up in the muscles during intense exercise, and eventually force you to slow or stop unless you can flush them out, or reduce the intensity (speed) of your running.

The Long Run gradually builds our stamina (and strength), and you will be surprised at how quickly your body adapts to runs of 10 miles or more, that would seem impossible at the start of your program.

Distance

How far should you run each week? This is hard to answer, as it depends on previous experience, and the time you have available. Also, runners respond in different ways to mileage. Some runners need to run very high mileage, whereas others can achieve similar results with a lower mileage, higher intensity program.

A sensible target for your first time would be 25-35 miles per week, at peak, with the longest run being 18 miles (no longer than 3 hours). For improving runners, from 35 miles up to 55 miles per week at peak will help build stamina and strength. Keep in mind that it can take several seasons to build up to weekly mileages above 55 miles, without over-training. I never ran more than 65 miles in one week, with the longest at 20 miles. More miles don't necessarily equate to faster times, and you can risk over-training if you try to ramp up mileage too quickly, so try to make your runs effective.

I met one runner (2:45 PB at 45 years old) who trained by running a fast 8-mile run 6 times per week, never more. Equally, I met another (2:38 PB at 42 years old) who said that he ran a marathon distance *every week* during training. Different philosophies, but both very successful. For most people, somewhere in the middle is best, with a mixture of shorter, faster runs combined with a weekly long run of a maximum (towards the end of the program) 18-20 miles. Also, try to avoid running for less than 30 minutes, as you get much more from a single 40-minute run than you would from 2 x 20-minute runs.

Warming up and down

I prefer not to warm up extensively to maximise running time, and I often do this through 'dynamic stretching' during the first mile (through lunging, exaggerated high knees, skipping). Most people who have taken part in sport will have been told to stretch, but you take care to avoid any stretching which does not simulate running movements in itself. Hence, don't yank your leg behind your back, bend double or over-lunge and put excessive strain on the calf muscles or hamstrings. Remember, a cheetah will go from standstill to 60mph and back again, and they don't warm up by stretching. Loosen up before, roll the neck and arms, take the legs through a range of dynamic motions, and then set off.

Warming down is essential though, in my view, and allow 5-10 minutes for this in each session. This will help to flush out lactates, and avoid tightening of muscles – this then makes the next day easier, and reduces the risk of injury.

If you feel any tightness in a specific area, and if this continues at a painful level during running, then stop, massage the area and slow the pace or shorten the run.

Be Specific

In short, you should focus your training on running. Cycling and swimming will help your general Cardiovascular (CV) fitness, and are not a bad thing in a training program when you need a rest from impact. However, a 10 mile cycle or 40 minutes of swimming will not improve your running strength. The most important thing is that you complete the **3 main sessions** (Long, Lactate, Speedwork), but if you can also fit extra sessions of running into your week, these will build muscle strength in key areas. Other activities will build your CV fitness, but will not help you to become a faster or stronger runner.

Avoid heavy weights, as you want to increase muscle strength, but not gain muscle mass or bulk. Hence, you might also want to avoid rowing and cross-training. If you do use the gym, focus instead on core exercises that build abdominal strength, or high repetition leg exercises (squats, calf raises).

For improving runners, I would recommend that you run exclusively, and aim to complete 5-6 sessions each week with 1 or 2 rest days, combining this with running-specific stretches and strength exercises.

Write down each session in summary - distance, course (hilly / flat), time. Even rest days and exercise days (weights, alternative activity) should be included, so you can compare and track your progress. You don't need to use a computer, just have a simple paper planner on the wall in the kitchen.

Programs

I ran my first marathon without a training program, and finished in 3:24. I ran 15 years later with a specific program, and finished in 2:44. The point is that following a proper training program makes a huge difference.

If you follow a proper training program, you will get better results, and enjoy the run more. It doesn't matter if it is the perfect training plan, just the fact that you are working to a plan with varied speed, distance, terrain and rest days will make a big difference.

Motivation

This can be hard to find some days, and it is vital to have something or someone external to motivate you. If you really enjoy your running, then mostly this will not be too difficult, although there is a difference between recreational running and working towards a goal. Below are some tips which might help:

- Find routes that you really enjoy, so that you look forward to these, and hence feel you have missed out if you cannot run

- Vary your routes, to maintain your interest. Look for different terrain (grass, road, beach, and pathway) and gradients flat and hilly.

- Find a time that suits you and stick to it. I like to run in the morning, so that during the training phase my morning run is something that **has** to be done before the day starts. If you run in the evening, then this is the final task of the before you can relax. What is important is that it becomes routine.

- 'Stick it on the Fridge' - set out your training program, print it off, and put it on the side of the fridge (or somewhere prominent in the kitchen). Each time you complete a run, you can tick it off, and also see your progress towards race day and this is very satisfying. I rarely miss a session during an 18 week program, and although speeds and distances aren't always on plan, it's 'on the fridge' and therefore has to be done.

- Remind yourself of the goal
    - Why are you doing this?
    - What do you want to achieve?
    - Picture how will you feel afterwards, when you have overcome this challenge (and this fantastic experience)

- Have heroes – it can help to read the background stories of great runners, what they have done and how they have reached their level. The stories of these runners are inspiring, and it's nice to feel that you are part of the same community. You can read more about these great runners online:

    - Haile Gebrselassie
    - Paula Radcliffe

- - Kerry Liam-Wilson
  - Mo Farah
  - Emil Zatopek
  - Paavo Nurmi
  - Jo Pavey
  - Steve Way
  - Scott Overall
  - Ron Hill

- Have heroes (Part II) – you can also be inspired by the stories of mere mortals, not just the elite runners. For example, people who have never run before, and have gone on to complete their first marathon, or maybe their first of many. Ask around locally, and speak to friends and contacts that run.

- Enjoy your running:

  - Don't obsess about the detail of every session
  - Find different routes, reverse them, get off road
  - Run with a partner or others in a group

- Train with others, with a club or have a trainer – naturally it is harder to skip sessions when you are running with others, and a good trainer will help set out a sensible program and help during hard times

- Play around – the concept of 'Fartlek' or 'Fahrtspielen' (meaning speed-play) was introduced after some success with improving strength in runners. Essentially, you can change your speed, cadence, sprint in bursts, lunge or skip – interspersed with periods of 'normal' running

- Place your running shoes in the corridor to act as a reminder, or lay out your gear the night before, so that you are ready to go at short notice

- Make a mental note, or a note in your diary, of your intended runs for the following day

- If you are travelling or cannot get out due to other circumstances, then you can substitute a treadmill run, but try to limit the time spent to less than an hour. Treadmills do not exactly replace a 'normal' run, and if over-used can cause injury from the abnormal impact.

Tapering

My advice is to taper from your *maximum mileage* by 25-30% per week. I prefer a 2-week taper, general advice is from 1 week to 3 weeks.

This will feel very odd!

You might find it unnerving and too hard to taper for 3 weeks, but in any case you must be well-rested prior to the race. The benefits are huge and you must keep the faith. Do not run more than 10 miles in a single session less than 5 days prior to your race. If your maximum mileage is 50 miles, then you would run 35-38 miles in the penultimate week, and 25-30 miles in the final week, majority being concentrated into the first half of this week.

Do not run on the final 2 days before race day, other than perhaps a short 2-3 mile if you really must, at a very gentle pace, followed by stretches. I find this helps calm the nerves a little, and prepares you for the race.

Avoiding Injury

Injury is a natural risk as you are putting the body (and in particular the legs, ankles and feet) under high levels of stress.

The normal pattern of muscle and tendon injury goes something like this –

1. 'Hmm, my Achilles / Calf / Hamstring feels tight today'
2. 'That's strange, when I ran again today, my Achilles / Calf / Hamstring was still really tight. Must do some stretches'
3. 'Argh, I've torn / pulled my Achilles / Calf / Hamstring'

Basically, there are usually warning signs that you are heading for an injury, and hence it can be avoided in many cases. Naturally, this is easier said than done, particularly when trying to separate a 'warning' ache from general aches and pains.

You must balance this against the training program, and whilst feeling tired is quite natural, ongoing tightness, stiffness or pain in a specific area is a sign that you need to do something. You might consider the following:

- Taking an extra rest day – the negative effect of 2-3 consecutive rest days over a full program is minimal, and if you have rest days already in your program this is easy

- Ramping up to higher mileage, or higher intensity very slowly, over a number of weeks

- Considering your footwear – is it old, and does the cushioning offer sufficient protection against impact

- Dynamic stretching after your runs – this should in any case be part of the program, but you might also want to add gentle stretches each morning, regardless of your running schedule

- Avoiding hard surfaces such as road / pavement, and reducing the amount of hill work as this puts strain on calves and Achilles

- Reducing the intensity (speed and distance) a little in the program – so rather than increasing these each week, you maintain the previous week's level

- Having a sports massage, or being adjusted by a professional chiropractor – this is good practice in any case, once or twice during the program

- Reducing your stride length (ie. increasing your cadence – the number of times you step each minute) – to avoid banging down on each stride

Plantar Fasciitis – generally only gets better with rest, and you might need to do this. If not too severe then change to softer surfaces and cut out fast runs for a session or two. Stretching can help, using a foot roller.

Achilles Heel – pay close attention, as an injury here can mean long-term inaction. If it is sore, avoid hill work and intense speed. If you are trying to shift to a lighter shoe, revert to heavier cushioning / normal drop (rear to front).

Hamstrings and Calf muscles – make sure you have a light warm up, and a proper warm down with a selection of leg stretches.

Runner's Knee – can be caused by the wrong footwear, and again if severe then switch to an alternative exercise to maintain CV fitness before returning to running.

Generally, you need to listen to your body, and increase intensity and mileage gradually.

Benchmarking

- Tune up races – these are a good way of evaluating your progress, and giving you a focus away from the program of training. A 10k or half marathon is the ideal distance, and the race should be comfortably spaced away from your actual race (by at least 3 weeks). This can give you a useful guide to your expected marathon time, using the calculations mentioned earlier.
- Yasso 800s – the Yasso method is well known, and based on my experience quite accurate. You set out to run 10 x 800m sets in a time (in minutes) equal to your intended time for the marathon (in hours), with an interval equal to the set time between each. For example, if you are setting out to run a 4:15 marathon

(4 hours, 15 minutes), then you try to run 10 sets of 800m in a time of 4:15 (4 minutes 15 seconds) for each set, with an equal rest interval of 4:15 between each. If you can do this, then you are on the right track.

- Measured half marathon – if you have a known route, ideally flat and firm, then you can push yourself on one of the pace runs in your program for 13.1 miles. Take this time, and multiply by 2, then add 15-20 minutes to give your expected marathon time.
- If you have completed several marathons, half marathons and 10k races before, you might also be able to assess whether you are a 'fast' runner, or an 'endurance' runner. My method is to compare your best race times in each event to the world record, and work out how many percentage points above this you rank. So, if your marathon time is 3:15 and the world record is 2:03 (approx.) then you are 158.5% of the world record. Do the same for 10k and half marathon, and if you are closer to WR in the shorter distances, then focus on your endurance training; if you are closer in the longer distances, then focus on speedwork.

7. Sample Training Programs

For the purposes of these sample programs, it is important that you have completed some longer runs, and have an idea of your intended race pace (or finish time).

Slow means deliberately slowing your pace to a comfortable level where you can breathe and talk easily. This should be 1:30 – 2:00 minutes per mile slower than race pace. Around 60% maximal effort if you track this through heart rate (for this, you need to have calculated your theoretical maximum heart rate).

Medium would be within 1 minute per mile of your intended race pace. So if your target pace is 8:00 minutes per mile for the race, this should be 8:00 – 9:00 minutes per mile. Around 75% maximal effort.

Fast would be between 30 and 60 seconds per mile faster than your race pace. Around 90% maximal effort.

For the Beginner Program, Days 2 / 5 / 7 are optional runs and for Intermediate Days 5 / 7 are optional; but I would strongly recommend trying to make at least one of these in the early part of the program, and all of them during the weeks 13-16. However, use your common sense, and if the body is telling you to rest then you need to listen.

Sample beginner training program

BEGINNER	Day 1	Day 2	Day 3	Day 4	Day 5	Day 6	Day 7
Week 1	3m slow	2m slow	3m medium	-	3m slow	6m slow	2m slow
Week 2	3m slow	2m slow	3m medium	-	3m slow	7m slow	2m slow
Week 3	3m medium	2m slow	4m medium	-	3m slow	8m slow	3m slow
Week 4	3m medium	3m slow	4m medium	-	3m slow	8m slow	3m slow
Week 5	3 x 1m fast	3m slow	5m medium	-	3m slow	10m slow	3m slow
Week 6	3 x 1m fast	3m slow	5m medium	-	3m slow	10m slow	3m slow
Week 7	6 x 800 fast	3m slow	5m at race pace	-	3m slow	12m slow	3m slow
Week 8	3 x 1m fast	3m slow	6m at race pace	-	3m slow	14m slow	3m slow
Week 9	6 x 800 fast	3m slow	6m at race pace	-	3m slow	10m slow	3m slow
Week 10	3 x 1m fast	3m slow	6m at race pace	-	3m slow	16m slow	3m slow
Week 11	6 x 800 fast	3m slow	7m at race pace	-	3m slow	18m slow	3m slow
Week 12	4 x 1m fast	3m slow	7m at race pace	-	3m slow	14m slow	3m slow
Week 13	6 x 800 fast	3m slow	7m at race pace	-	3m slow	18m slow	3m slow
Week 14	4 x 1m fast	3m slow	8m at race pace	-	3m slow	14m slow	3m slow
Week 15	6 x 800 fast	3m slow	8m at race pace	-	3m slow	20m slow	3m slow
Week 16	3 x 1m fast	3m slow	8m at race pace	-	3m slow	13m slow	3m slow
Week 17	3 x 1m fast	3m slow	6m medium	-	2m slow	8m slow	-
Week 18	2m + fast 1m	4m slow	4m medium	-	2m slow	Easy jog	RACE DAY
	INTERVAL	OPTION	PACE	REST	OPTION	LONG	OPTION

- 1m, 2m, 3m = 1 mile, 2 mile, 3 mile and so on
- 800 = 800m

Sample intermediate training program

INTERMEDIATE	Day 1	Day 2	Day 3	Day 4	Day 5	Day 6	Day 7
Week 1	3m slow	2m slow	3m medium	-	3m slow	6m slow	2m slow
Week 2	3m slow	2m slow	3m medium	-	3m slow	7m slow	2m slow
Week 3	3m medium	3m slow	4m medium	-	3m slow	8m slow	3m slow
Week 4	3m medium	4m slow	4m medium	-	3m slow	8m slow	3m slow
Week 5	3 x 1m fast	4m slow	5m medium	-	3m slow	10m slow	3m slow
Week 6	3 x 1m fast	4m slow	5m medium	-	3m slow	10m slow	3m slow
Week 7	6 x 800 fast	4m slow	5m at race pace	-	3m slow	12m slow	3m slow
Week 8	3 x 1m fast	4m slow	6m at race pace	-	3m slow	14m slow	3m slow
Week 9	6 x 800 fast	4m slow	6m at race pace	-	3m slow	10m slow	3m slow
Week 10	3 x 1m fast	4m slow	6m at race pace	-	3m slow	16m slow	3m slow
Week 11	6 x 800 fast	4m slow	7m at race pace	-	4m slow	18m slow	3m slow
Week 12	4 x 1m fast	4m slow	7m at race pace	-	4m slow	14m slow	3m slow
Week 13	6 x 800 fast	5m slow	7m at race pace	-	4m slow	20m slow	3m slow
Week 14	6 x 1000 fast	5m slow	8m at race pace	-	4m slow	16m slow	3m slow
Week 15	6 x 1000 fast	5m slow	9m at race pace	-	4m slow	20m slow	3m slow
Week 16	4 x 1m fast	5m slow	10m at race pace	-	4m slow	14m slow	3m slow
Week 17	3 x 1m fast	4m slow	6m medium	-	2m slow	8m slow	-
Week 18	2m + fast 1m	4m slow	4m medium	-	2m slow	Easy jog	RACE DAY
	INTERVAL	EASY	PACE	REST	OPTION	LONG	OPTION

- 1m, 2m, 3m = 1 mile, 2 mile, 3 mile and so on
- 800, 1000 = 800m, 1000m

Sample advanced training program

ADVANCED	Day 1	Day 2	Day 3	Day 4	Day 5	Day 6	Day 7
Week 1	3m slow	2m slow	3m medium	-	3m slow	6m slow	2m slow
Week 2	3m slow	2m slow	3m medium	-	3m slow	7m slow	2m slow
Week 3	3m medium	3m slow	4m medium	-	3m slow	8m slow	3m slow
Week 4	3m medium	4m slow	4m medium	-	3m slow	8m slow	3m slow
Week 5	3 x 1m fast	4m slow	5m medium	-	3m slow	10m slow	3m slow
Week 6	3 x 1m fast	4m slow	5m medium	-	3m slow	10m slow	3m slow
Week 7	6 x 800 fast	4m slow	5m at race pace	-	3m slow	12m slow	3m slow
Week 8	3 x 1m fast	4m slow	6m at race pace	-	4m slow	14m slow	3m slow
Week 9	6 x 800 fast	4m slow	6m at race pace	-	4m slow	10m slow	3m slow
Week 10	3 x 1m fast	5m slow	7m at race pace	-	5m slow	16m slow	3m slow
Week 11	8 x 800 fast	5m slow	8m at race pace	-	5m slow	18m slow	3m slow
Week 12	6 x 1000 fast	5m slow	9m at race pace	-	5m slow	14m slow	3m slow
Week 13	10 x 800 fast	6m slow	10m at race pace	-	6m slow	20m slow	3m slow
Week 14	5 x 1m fast	6m slow	11m at race pace	-	6m slow	16m slow	3m slow
Week 15	6 x 1000 fast	7m slow	12m at race pace	-	7m slow	20m slow	3m slow
Week 16	10 x 800 fast	7m slow	1/2 marathon at race pace	-	7m slow	14m slow	3m slow
Week 17	3 x 1m fast	4m slow	6m medium	-	2m slow	8m slow	-
Week 18	2m + fast 1m	4m slow	4m medium	-	2m slow	Easy jog	RACE DAY
	INTERVAL	EASY	PACE	REST	EASY	LONG	EASY

- 1m, 2m, 3m = 1 mile, 2 mile, 3 mile and so on
- 800, 1000 = 800m, 1000m

8. Running technique

Strike!

Much has been written on this topic recently with regards to 'strike' (the way in which the foot contacts the ground), and how this can affect speed and risk of injury.

If you are running for the first time, the most important factor is your footwear, but if you naturally strike with the midfoot or forefoot then this is good. If you are a natural heel-striker, you need to decide whether to continue in this style or try to move towards the forefoot. My personal opinion, without wishing to join the debate, is that if you are natural in this style and have not been injured, then you should maintain it for your first time.

For more experienced runners, you might consider aiming to spend the majority (but not all) of your time during the race on the midfoot and forefoot, which if you are a natural heel-striker, will require that you make some fine adjustments.

My 'natural' running style tends towards a heel strike, and I had run in this way for years without serious injury. However, at higher speeds you will move towards the forefoot in any case, as the body is more angled forward. In trying to develop my speed and reduce my times, I spent some time (18 months) adjusting my style, so that I spent *more time* on the forefoot. There are 3 main reasons for this:

- In order to improve speed, the natural rebound from a forefoot technique should drive your leg into the next stride

- Over the course of a marathon, if you are able to alter your strike (and cadence) subtly during the race, you will share the work across a broader group of muscles, reducing the fatigue in a specific area

- Once you have built the strength to run the majority of the race on the midfoot / forefoot, you can drop to a lighter-cushioned shoe, reducing critical weight in this area

Note – I did not run forefoot for an entire race, but would generally start in this style, and allow myself periods on the heel, particularly when descending as this is more natural on downhills.

If you have always been a heel striker, you should be very careful when changing to a forefoot style. Even over short distances (less than 3 miles), you can easily over-stress calf muscles and Achilles tendons, and quickly cause injury. You need time to build the strength in the calf muscles and arches of the foot, and accustom the Achilles to being extended more than normal (since the extension is smaller in a heel striking technique). The debate seems to be quite entrenched, with a narrative that heel-striking is 'bad' and forefoot running is 'good'. However, there are many recreational runners that are very fast, and remain injury-free with a lifelong heel-strike technique.

In my view, it is not sensible to combine a change in style with *'barefoot' (low cushioned, 'zero-drop') running shoes.* You can train and adjust to a forefoot technique equally well in 'normal' cushioned shoes, with the added benefit that if you should drop back into a heel strike pattern during the session you will have adequate cushioning.

My recommendation is to build up very carefully over months (if you have this much time), starting with periods of forefoot running (no more than 1km at a time, 1-2 times in a session). The running style is coupled with a more upright posture, which in itself opens up the chest, and generates high-knee 'cycling' legs. However, if you only have 14 weeks, and have no current injury problems, I would suggest that you stay as you are. It is just my view....

Cadence

Firstly, measure your natural cadence. This will be somewhere in the range 160-200 strikes per minute. The simple way is to count the number of steps you complete in 30 seconds, and then double it. Mine sits at around 185 per minute on flat tarmac.

Once you have established your natural rhythm, experiment with a slightly faster cadence (shorter stride), then measure this. Repeat the exercise with a slower cadence (longer stride), then measure this. Now you have your range. Mine varies between 180 and 190, and surprisingly a small change of +/-5 strikes per minute feels quite different.

If you can maintain your stride length, but increase your cadence, then you will increase your speed. Hence, you should focus on running at a slightly higher cadence (2-3 strikes per minute) than your natural rhythm, and in time you will come up to this. If you can maintain your stride length, through training with lunges, strength exercises, and your weekly running program then you will become faster.

Also, during a marathon, you should shift your cadence subtly during the race, as this naturally changes your strike and stride length, and will work different muscles in the foot and leg. I do this by running a higher cadence, with pronounced forefoot strike on climbs and flat sections, and a slower cadence with larger strides (and heel strike) when descending. You can actually feel the change as certain muscles are rested during these descents.

Breathing

When you first start training, you might find that you are short of breath or struggle to get into a comfortable rhythm. I find this difficulty with swimming, although with running it seemed to happen naturally. However, I still needed to make improvements to maximise the potential to oxygenate the muscles.

Don't stop – you will get into a habitual stop-start pattern that is difficult to break. Slow down, but keep running, however slowly this might be.

Breathe through both mouth and nose. You can train for this by breathing in through the nose and out through the mouth for 30-40 cycles, then normally, then vice versa, when running.

Control – try to manage your breathing, so that it fits with the rhythm and pace at which you are running. It is quite difficult at first, but if you are aware that you are honking air, then try to get this under control again.

Warm up breathing – stand straight, with head raised and chin tucked. Place the hands in prayer position under the neck and concentrate on breathing into this point. Next, place the hands on the rib cage, circling them with forefinger and thumb, and again focus on breathing into this point. Finally, place the hands on the stomach, and breathe into this point.

Posture – make sure that you are not hunching or dropping your head. Hunching will compress the ribs and lower abdomen, and dropping your head puts pressure on the windpipe, making it harder to breathe freely. Try to remain upright, with head held and looking forward.

Advancing runners – you can play around with holding your breath for short periods, and then 'catching up', or consciously trying to breathe more slowly even during harder efforts. This will encourage the body to take advantage of the depleted oxygen available, and improve conversion when you return to your natural pattern.

Posture and position

Avoid the assumption that your normal gait is the best because that is how you 'naturally' run. The ideal condition is where you can maintain your speed with minimal effort from the arms, a regular stride length, and minimal vertical movement (bounce).

Run tall - aim to be upright, with the head raised (chin up and tucked), and shoulders relaxed but not slumping.

Don't rotate excessively - arms should be tucked in, not flailing around, so that they can assist in propelling you forward without wasting energy. You do not need to pump your arms like a sprinter, but they should be used.

Don't bounce excessively - this is wasted energy. If you can imagine a line at eye level, you are trying to keep at this height through the running cycle. Of course, your head will go up and down, but minimising it makes your more efficient. The rebound of each stride should be taking you forward, not upwards.

Avoid over-striding – a good way to change this is to slightly increase your cadence (strikes per minute), as your stride length will then decrease, bringing the ankle in under the knee as you strike.

Avoid under-striding – this of course differs for runners with different leg lengths, but under-striding increases the amount of contact with the ground, and therefore can slow your pace (or increase the effort required).

Good striding exercises involve running a fixed number of paces in a fixed distance.

Have a friend video you running from the front and from the side, and watch it back to analyse any areas for improvement.

9. Nutrition

As a general rule, you will need to increase your intake of protein and carbohydrate during a training program. You should also make sure you get a good supply of good 'fats', as your body needs to get used to burning fat alongside carbohydrate.

Generally, for both weight management endurance and power, I tried to focus on a relatively low carb, higher protein diet. I also tried to eliminate monosaccharides (simple sugar, such as from sweet drinks, or sugar itself). There are complete books on 'primal' diets for runners, and whilst I didn't go this far, it makes good sense to follow the rules below:

AVOID OR REDUCE - Bread, Crisps, Cakes, Biscuits, Pastry, Dairy, Potatoes, White Pasta and RIce

INTRODUCE – Fruit, Vegetables, Fish, Lean Meat, Nuts, Porridge Oats, Wholemeal Pasta, Low-Fat Plain Yoghurt

---

Carbohydrate

It is often said that "you need to load up on your carbs", but take this with a pinch of (low-sodium) salt. You will of course burn carb during your training sessions, but try to rebalance the carb you have used, without going too crazy. For example, you don't need to follow each session with 3 slices of toast and peanut butter, a chocolate bar and an Isotonic 'sports drink'. Otherwise you are simply teaching your body that it can burn lots of carb, and that this will then be replaced. The body gets used to this pattern – burn carb, replace carb, repeat.

This means you are teaching the body only to use carbohydrate, not **carbohydrate alongside fat**, and this 'dual-fuel' supply is essential for good marathon running. Running with depleted levels of carbohydrate trains the body to rely more on fat as a source of fuel.

Imagine a car with 2 power sources – petrol, and electrical battery. The petrol converts rapidly into energy when power is needed, but is not very efficient. The battery is very efficient, but is limited to the amount of power it can deliver. By analogy, if you accelerate quickly, climb a hill, or want to go very fast then the car prefers to use petrol. If you are coasting, going slowly or descending, then the car can switch to the battery source.

When running the same is true – more powerful, faster activity requires a greater proportion of carb burning, whereas at lower levels a larger proportion of fat is burnt. Fat contains more than double the calories per gram, compared to carbohydrate, so it is essential that you unlock and use these stores of fat.

Analysis of glycogen and fat consumption at varying levels of intensity:

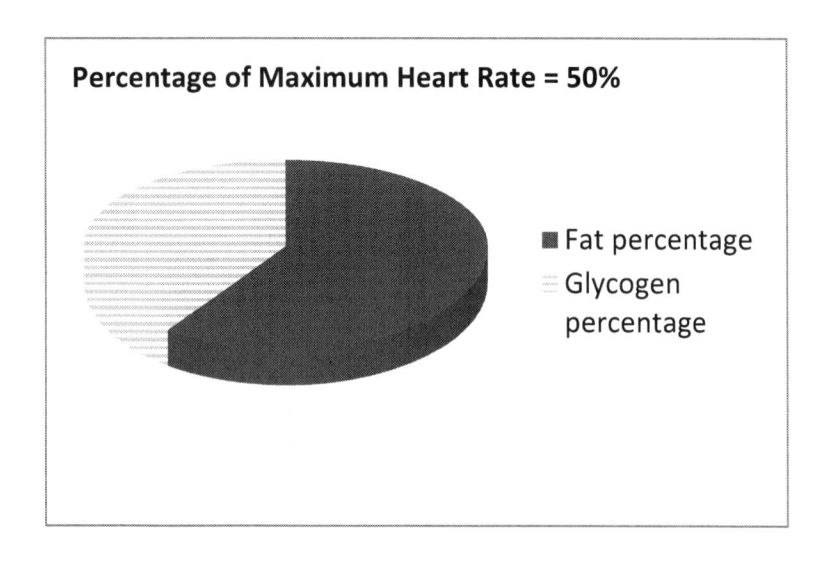

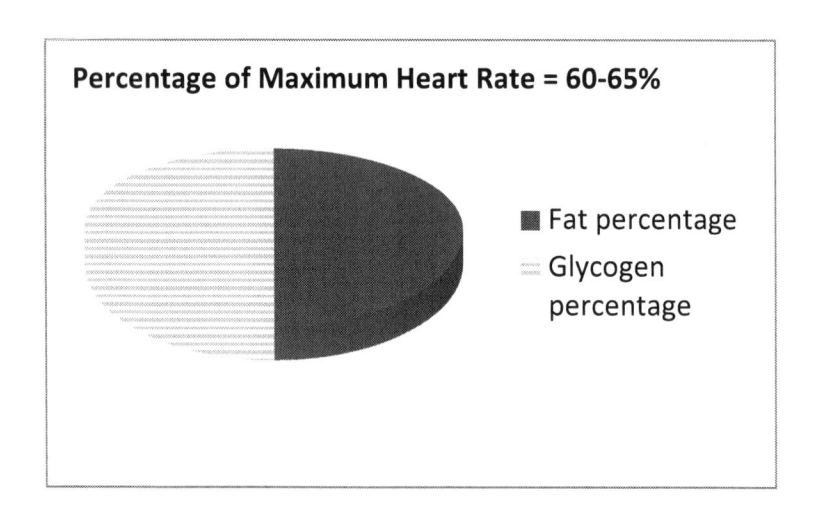

Percentage of Maximum Heart Rate = 50%

- Fat percentage
- Glycogen percentage

Percentage of Maximum Heart Rate = 60-65%

- Fat percentage
- Glycogen percentage

Percentage of Maximum Heart Rate = 80-85%

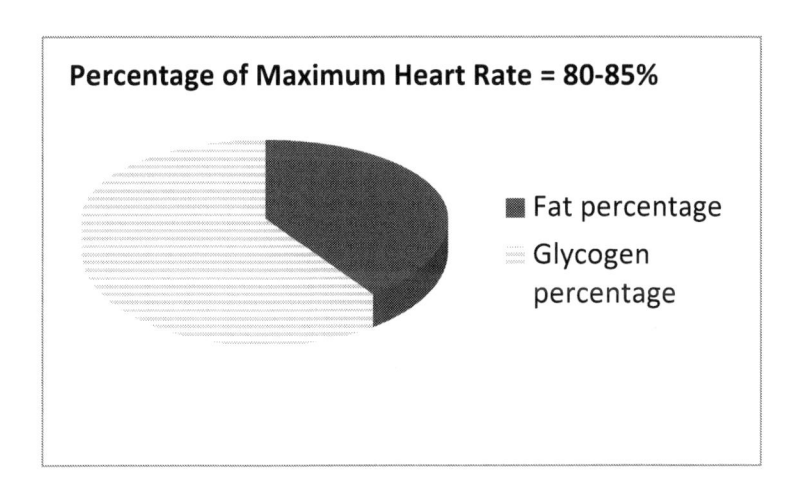

- Fat percentage
- Glycogen percentage

In a marathon, you are trying to run at a moderately hard level, so the proportion of carbohydrate used is relatively high. The problem here is that your 'petrol tank' is not large enough to store enough carb to run the full marathon at the desired intensity. This can lead to the so-called 'Wall' in later stages, or rather the point at which you have stopped metabolising efficiently and will have to slow down or stop (but more of this later).

Hence, you must train the body to burn a higher proportion of fat at higher levels of intensity and this is achieved through training. This will maintain your stores of carbohydrate, and allow you to maintain a higher intensity to the finish line.

The first method is running around the 'Lactate Threshold' (LT). This is the point at which the proportion of carbohydrate to fat suddenly increases. Of course, this cannot be measured outside the lab, so a good benchmark is around 80% maximum pace, moderate hard breathing (unable to hold a sustained conversation). These LT runs should be built into the schedule, with distances from 6 – 10 miles, increasing in distance as you work through the program. There is much evidence that sustained runs over 10-12 weeks around this threshold will increase the LT – ie. raise the level of intensity at which the metabolism of carbohydrate suddenly increases - and therefore allow you to run at the same level of intensity as earlier in your training program, but burning a greater proportion of fat. This preserves your carbohydrate stores.

The second method which I firmly believe to be effective is 'running on empty'. Essentially, you run early in the morning, prior to eating. I wouldn't suggest going for more than an hour, and only on your medium pace runs, however I have previously run over 2 hours on nothing more than a glass of water after waking. What is happening? The body has residual carbohydrate stored in the body, from the previous evening, and when you train under these conditions, the body will seek out other stores of energy (namely fat) alongside the carbohydrate available. I found over time (10-12 weeks) that I became much more able to run for sustained periods without carbohydrate before, during or after a session. Naturally, when you then come to race day, you will have eaten in the morning, and will take on gels and carb during the race so your body is being 'well-fed' on race day, compared to these training sessions.

Aim to eat 'complex carbs' post-training and as part of your diet, as these take longer for the body to metabolise and provide a longer lasting source of energy.

Good carbohydrate:

- Sweet potato
- Other vegetables
- Quinoa
- Barley
- Brown rice
- Rolled oats
- Wholemeal pasta
- Fruit but not excessive amounts

Fat

Fat is really important for good endurance - but be careful about the type of fat. Avoid fatty meat, and saturated fats.

Unlike distances up to half marathon, it is essential to build the capacity of the body to metabolise fat. The body can go for hundreds of miles on its fat reserves, whereas you cannot store enough carbohydrate in your liver and muscles to complete a marathon! In short, you must be burning a significant proportion of **fat** at your intended race-pace, otherwise you will used up your carbohydrate too quickly. This leads to a chain of events that will end with you having to slow or stop, normally around 18-20 miles – this is the so-called 'wall'.

- Avocados
- Eggs
- Dark Chocolate
- Cheese
- Nuts
- Seeds
- Coconut
- Palm oil (responsibly sourced)
- Oily Fish

Protein

Protein is a **vital** rebuilding block for muscles, after hard or long sessions.

A higher protein diet is essential both during the program, and immediately after a session and I always try to get protein back into the body **less than 60** minutes after a session. If you miss this window, it will take longer for the muscles to recover and hence affect the next day(s) training.

The reason for this is that protein in the muscles stressed and broken down during intensive or long training sessions, and consequently needs to be repaired. Ideally, as quickly as possible after a session, to allow the muscles to be used again at a moderate to high level the following day.

It can be a bit difficult to throw together a rice and grilled chicken meal, let alone eat it after a hard session, but a protein shake can provide a quick and easy solution.

- Eggs
- Chicken
- Fish
- Nuts
- Baked beans
- Bean salad
- Soya
- Quorn
- Protein powder

If you like eggs, they are a true superfood so try to bring these in as bulk when you are hungry. They are also great after long runs, as they are a great source of protein. Also, you can still have sweet treats like biscuits and chocolate, but try to make the biscuits yourself, and stick to dark chocolate in limited amounts.

Other Tips

- Beetroot Juice – this contains Nitric Oxide (NO) which seems to assist the cells metabolise oxygen, making for faster sessions, and quicker recovery. The science behind this is still in debate, but I am a believer
- Pre-made snacks – a great way to get healthy fruit and nuts into the system, and still feeling you have had a sweet reward (such as a rolled oat, honey and chopped dried fruit biscuit)
- Alcohol – within moderation, I don't see a problem with this, as my friends will testify. The rule is that you should be able to manage a hard session the following day, so take it easy if your plan requires this, or move the hard sessions around if you have a fixed social event
- Hydration – many people like to run with fluid on board during training. I don't in general except when the run is approaching 2 hours or more, but you should do what suits you, and make sure you drink plenty of water before and after
- Vitamin supplements – if you feel you need these, they can't hurt, but the only thing I would take as a supplement is Vitamin C near a race to try to stave off colds

10. Race day

Basics

- Prepare your kit and race day bag the night before
- Make sure your kit is familiar, and has been tested
- Get plenty of sleep the night before
- Leave ample time to reach the start
- If you have a GPS watch, make sure it is fully charged, and consider also having a back-up stopwatch
- Visualise the distance, and respect it
- Know the route and have your race plan worked out
- Decide what you are doing with clothing, and make sure you are warm enough at the start of the race, even if this means throwing away old clothes, or use the bagging service
- Use the bathroom
- Make your way to the line around 10-15 minutes before gun time

Start line

- Don't panic about trying to be close to the start line – the chip will activate as you cross the mat, so you will not 'lose' time getting to the start. The chip time and gun time will be listed for you, and chip time is the important one (unless you plan to win)

- Hence, pick a position which reflects your anticipated finish time – there is nothing worse than being pushed aside by faster runners for the first 5 miles, or similarly being held up as you try to make your way through a crowd because you have started too far back
- If you are throwing clothes away, keep these until the last minute, and then discard carefully to the side – often these are collected and recycled

Pace

- There are 3 different profiles for racing:

    - Positive split – second half is slower than first half. This is standard for most runners, with a built in 'fade' as you tire. It can suggest that you have gone too fast for the first half, but unless you are quite experienced, I would advise this strategy when planning your split times, allowing the second half to be slower than the first by 10 mins (3 hour target), 15 mins (4 hour target), 20 mins (5 hour target)

    - Neutral – good strategy for more experienced runners, as you try to maintain a constant pace throughout the race. It will be difficult to get to this on your first race, without going too slowly or quickly, but my best races have been very even splits (1:22 / 1:22 and 1:22 / 1:23)

- o Negative split – second half faster than first half, for very experienced runners, although you might also manage this if you are being cautious on the first half and then have some fuel in the tank at the end. It is a nice way to race, if you are not obsessed about time for your first race – start slowly and build up

- It will help to calculate your average pace and intended time at various points through the race. I have a complete breakdown of *all splits* jotted on my hand, but this is for runners aiming to go faster. If you have a GPS watch, then you can just monitor the average pace, and check if you are on target

- If you have followed a training plan, and mostly met the times and mileages, then you will have a fairly good idea of your target time. You will not suddenly shave 30 minutes off, and equally you will not 'blow up' if you set out a sensible pace and maintain this

- Don't go off like a greyhound – this will hurt you at 16-20 miles, and might even lead to you stopping. If it is your first time, then start below your intended pace and build up

  - Base your racing pace on your 18-20 mile long run pace. On race day, you will always find something extra, but there is a limit to this. If you can run 18 miles at a certain pace in training, I would say you can do the same for 26 miles on race day

- If you have a certain pace in mind, then try to find experienced runners who are aiming for the same, or run with designated 'pace' markers (for larger events, they will be holding up a large sign with the finish time on it)

Fuelling

- In my view, carb-loading 3-4 days prior to the event is not necessary. You will just be building fat, as the body converts excess carbohydrate into fat and then stores this. Instead, eat normally (protein and carbohydrate) leading up to the race, and on the evening before have a higher-carbohydrate meal, at a generous serving size.

- The morning of the race is more important. Remember that you cannot store enough glycogen to complete the race, so you should aim to take on what you can between 4 and 1 hours from the start of the race. Generally, you should aim to have a substantial breakfast, including 3-4 bananas, porridge, toast and jam or honey, dried fruit or chocolate, and eggs (as these help stabilise all the sweet foods and fruit). Then you can top up with bananas, and sipped sweet drinks (for energy), and water (to hydrate). If you struggle to eat this amount due to nerves, increase your intake the evening before. I tend to drink a bottle of flat Coke before the race, although I changed this for Irn Bru when I ran Loch Ness.

- Only eat things that you would normally eat at home. During the race your body is in stress, so don't add to it by eating unfamiliar foods.

- This rule is also important if you take any fruit, energy bars or gels during the race. Eat and drink only things you've tested during training, as you might find that gels upset your stomach. Bear in mind that bananas are difficult to eat during the race, and won't help you after 20 miles as they take an hour to digest. So you can take fruit early in the race, and keep the gels for later.

- Fruit, gels and water are normally provided, but carry some additional fuel on board – many options, but sweets, energy bars and gels (as mentioned) are popular. Belts are ideal for this, as the pockets in shorts are often limited in size. Experiment during training, to find the right balance, so that you are not running 26 miles with a dozen energy gels bouncing around your waist. It's annoying, and slows you down.

- Take water at *every station.* Easy to pass by without stopping, but keep in mind that you will lose around 1 litre (nearly 2 pints) of water every hour – so over 3-5 hours.....you must take water on board. Practice drinking from a cup whilst running, and note that even if you lose 2 seconds whilst slowing down to take a proper drink, it will be in your favour at the end of the race. You don't need to crowd in with the other runners at the first opportunity to get water. The stations are normally 75-100m long, so you can find a space further along the station where you are less obstructed and don't need to slow your pace or risk collision.

3 Phases

- The marathon is different from other running distances, and I normally like to break the race down into 3 stages

    - First stage – up to 15 miles; generally you should be comfortable over this distance and whilst you will feel the effort, you will also be enjoying the atmosphere and experience. It is very important to maintain your target pace here, and not go too fast. Also, to remember to hydrate as this will reward you later in the race. Lock into your pace, find your rhythm, fuel regularly and hydrate (either through sipping if you are carrying water, or at the water stations). Make sure you are sticking to your race plan, as during this phase you should still be fairly able to calculate your pace, and pay attention. It gets harder after 15 miles, as the mind becomes distracted.

    - Second stage – from around 15-20 miles. This for me is that hardest part of the race in many ways. You are now getting to the limit of your peak training distances, and this can have a psychological effect. You will also be tired. Often the combination of fatigue, inexperience of this distance, and uncertainty about finishing can lead you to slow or stop. Unless you are really struggling, try not to do this, as you will not get back up to speed again without serious effort. It might signal the end of the race, and a slow walk home. Stay positive, and remind yourself that you are now counting down the miles to the finish (after the halfway point). During this phase of the race, you are most likely to experience 'The Wall'. Personally, I think of this more as a slope than a wall. A wall makes you stop, whereas a slope just makes it harder, and in this case if you have followed a training plan and stuck to your target pace, there is no reason to stop. *Note that in many cases, people do not experience this at all.* As I said, it is just a combination of fatigue, and normally an increase in 'perceived intensity' during this phase. If you can block it out, and push through this to 20 miles, then you will almost certainly complete the race. There are various distraction techniques – 'outward' facing (where you think about external things, such as what other runners are wearing, the faces of the people in the crowd, what you might drink or eat when you finish the race), 'numerical' (I am constantly calculating and re-calculating my pace, last 5 mile speed, distance to the next mile marker, projected finish time, and so on), or 'internal' (positive examples would focus on your legs springing, your arms pumping, the rhythm of your breathing)

- Third stage – from 20 miles to finish. For me, the 20 mile (32km) point is a major marker in the race. If you tend to think in miles, then you have passed 20 and from here will be counting down from 6 to zero. If you work in kilometres, from 10 to zero, *but of course in both cases, you now only have a 10k to do* – and you will have done many of these during training. Say this to yourself in your head, and start to visualise what you will do at the finish. It feels great, and you will quite likely feel a lift in energy, after the grind of the previous phase. The running during this phase will also feel different, as the body continues to fatigue, but the mind takes over and starts to win the battle. There is still a small chance that you could blow up, but it is quite unlikely at this stage – however, don't forget to hydrate, fuel, and maintain an even pace. You are close to the finish, but not that close. Once you reach 23-24 miles, other than rare late-stage injuries, you will get home. Enjoy these last few miles, as this is the best part of the race. Generally, if there is a crowd, the support will be greatest here, so take advantage of this as you focus completely on finishing strongly.

At the end of the race, you will feel exhilarated and exhausted. Most likely you will be greeted by friends and family, and a huge crowd of runners and spectators. Enjoy the moment, but don't forget to immediately re-hydrate with water and hot, sweet drinks, eat something tasty, and get warm. Take off any wet clothes, and change into some dry kit. Stretch out thoroughly, shake off, and if you can bear it gently jog up and down to prevent your muscles tightening up altogether.

Take a moment to reflect on what you enjoyed, where you felt good or bad, and whether your race went to plan. If you are planning further runs, this will help you with the next race.

If you have a GPS watch, then you should analyse your mile splits, as this can help to indicate where you might have pushed too hard, or struggled for some reason. Below is a breakdown of my mile splits from a previous race. I can track what I was doing each mile, and since this was a double loop, can compare my first lap to my second. Therefore, it gives me good information about my performance during the start, mid- and closing phase (the three phases).

Mile	Time (mins, secs)	Time decimal
1	6.15	6.25
2	6.09	6.15
3	6.00	6.00
4	6.01	6.02
5	6.20	6.33
6	6.43	6.72
7	7.22	7.37
8	5.56	5.93
9	5.49	5.81
10	6.06	6.10
11	6.13	6.22
12	6.19	6.33
13	6.06	6.10
14	6.17	6.28
15	6.03	6.05
16	6.00	6.00
17	6.15	6.25
18	6.27	6.45
19	7.14	7.23
20	6.02	6.03
21	5.50	5.83
22	6.00	6.00
23	6.13	6.22
24	6.14	6.23
25	6.04	6.07
26	6.11	6.18

You can see, for example, the climbing miles (5,6,7) in the first loop were slower than in the second loop (17,18,19). This was where I was trying to push on, and it can be useful to compare your split times to perceived effort during tune-up races, so you get a good feel for what it takes in terms of effort to attain a certain pace.

11. Going faster

Weights and Exercises

You are aiming to increase strength without building bulk, and this is best achieved through high repetition, low resistance exercises. I recommend the following, or certainly the arm, leg and abdomen exercises 3-4 times per week if possible.

Of these, **_abdominal exercises are the most important._** The muscles that lift your legs up and down and rotate the upper body as you run are all connecting into the abdominals, so building up your 'core' is vital to improving your speed.

- Upper body (arms) – 2-4kg range dumbbells, bicep curls x 40-50, tricep press x 10-20 – arm strength naturally helps, when you have to pump them back and forth for 26 miles.
- Running with very light resistance (1-2 kg extra weight, in backpack). Avoid using leg weights, or larger weight on the back, as this will mess with your style.
- Abdominals – there are too many variants of abdominal exercise to list, but I like the lying-flat leg raise (15-20 times, 2x repeats), basic crunch and cross-over crunch (right elbow to left knee, left elbow to right knee). Find a regime that works for you, and aim for around 50-100 total reps of all variants combined.
- Introduce high intensity short runs into your program
- Calf raises – stand with feet apart, and gently raise onto tiptoe, repeat 40-50. Add 5-10kg if you wish, and ideally if you can do this on a pavement edge, to over-extend, this is better.

- Quad exercises (squat, reaching squat) – stand with legs shoulder width apart, and crouch down into a low squat, then stand (10-20 repeats). Try this also on single legs, alternating, but do not squat as deep. Also, you can perform the single leg squat, but as you bend the standing leg, reach forward as if picking up a beach ball off the ground, then return to standing on one leg (10-20 repeats, each leg)
- Plyometrics (or jump training) – I can try to describe this, but best that you check it out on YouTube. Do it where nobody can see you.
- Yoga and stretching – make sure that you maximise your flexibility, as this will pay dividends in stride length and rebound. Take care not too overstretch – just remember to make it relevant movements that relate to running.
- Pilates – fantastic for posture, breathing, core strength – pretty much the best thing you can do other than running itself, or to complement your running.

Body mass

The game here is to reduce your weight, without losing strength, which is quite a challenge during a training program. You will probably get a little heavier at first with a higher intensity program as you gain muscle before you lose fat. Do not be alarmed! If you have tried the above exercise of running with extra weights, you will know how much difference 1 or 2 kilograms feels, so imagine how it will feel without this on board. If you can manage your carbs, keep your protein high, and avoid sugary treats you will very likely reach your minimum achievable weight. My normal weight ranges from 72-74kg, but during a training program I will get down to around 70-71kg prior to racing. Lighter than this for me seems to be impossible, so don't obsess about it. If you consciously try to lose weight through reduction of intake, you will likely lose strength, so you must eat plenty but eat well to achieve strength and weight-reduction.

12. Summing Up

There is no mystery to running a marathon. If you do the work, you will finish the race, and enjoy it.

The key to your success is to have a plan for training, and a plan for the race, and then follow this.

Remember these 9-steps, as you work through your training:

- HYDRATION – stay hydrated during and after training, and practice drinking on the move, at your race speed. It is harder than it sounds.
- FUELLING – the key to a good race is to eat plenty of complex carbs in the hours before the race, and to take in simple carbs during the race
- WEIGHT – if you can reduce your weight by a few per cent in training, without losing strength, this will make a significant difference to your performance
- SPEEDWORK – you must introduce an amount of shorter faster runs, and increase core and leg muscle strength if you want to improve your strength and speed
- WEIGHTS, PILATES AND YOGA – to go faster, build core strength in abdomen, and leg strength and flexibility in quads and calf muscles
- TECHNIQUE – run well, breathe well, and work hard at your running style, remembering that all excess movement and contact with ground is lost energy
- TAPER – you need plenty of rest in the final 2 weeks before your race, which means cutting your training by

25%, then another 25% compared to peak mileage, and getting plenty of sleep
- PACING – maintain a steady pace throughout the race, working to a pre-race plan, measured against course timers or a wristwatch.
- DIET – if you can mostly follow a diet that is high in protein, sensible on carb, and has a good level of healthy fats, this will boost your power to weight, and raise endurance levels

13. After the event

If you are a first-time runner, you should be feeling a massive sense of pride at what you have achieved. For improving runners, hopefully you obtained a PB, or some other goal (placing, landmark event), and if not that you enjoyed the race and learnt from it. And hopefully didn't get beaten by anyone running backwards dressed as a banana, or someone in a rhino-suit.

The mind and body have come together and carried you over 26.2 miles at running speed. It is an amazing achievement, whether you are a first-timer or a veteran.

Recovery

Immediately after the event, you will need to rest for a few days to a week. Some people recover faster than others, and generally this is linked to your experience. Nonetheless, whatever your level, you should expect to be stiff for several days, and lacking in power for a few weeks compared to your pre-race levels.

Have plenty of hot baths, or if you prefer hot showers, using the sprayer to direct hot water onto your calf muscles and thighs. Get someone to massage your feet and legs (if you can….) and consider having a professional sports massage or adjustment with a chiropractor. Most likely, your body will be out of line and will need re-setting.

I prefer to get back into gentle runs within a few days of the event, but if this does not appeal, you can also try swimming or cycling.

Reward yourself too with all the things you like to eat and drink, and maybe buy a new pair of running shoes….ready for the next event.

Maintenance

In the absence of a formal training program, and a target race, it will be hard to continue training. I try to set my next event in the diary before I complete the last one; otherwise it is easy to feel uncertain about what to do next. The next race could be 18 months away, but it will give you the momentum to continue.

Make arrangements to run the following weekend, with friends, so that you are committed to something. This will help you get back into your running, and if you only ever intended to do one marathon, it would be a shame to give up such a great sport.

Also remember, running is not all about racing. You should be in the best shape of your life, and want to maintain that level of fitness and health. Running makes you more alert and less tired, and there is something fantastic about being out in the open air, and just running…..

Enjoy it!

Adam

14. About the Author

I wanted to write this guide to try to answer all the questions I have been asked over the last 5 years, and put down some of things I have picked up from many experienced runners. Also, because I am taking a year out, I needed something else to work on. I love to run, and to talk about running, and I've been lucky enough to swap stories with many runners, some with huge experience and others training for their first race.

I've been asked many times to provide training plans and tips, as in turn I have skimmed these from other runners. Hopefully I have inspired a few non-runners to take up the sport, and complete their first race along the way, whether a 5k, 10k, half or full marathon.

I am not an Elite runner, and I wouldn't call myself an obsessive runner, who has to get out every day and run for endless miles. But I do like to run, and I made it my main sport. I wanted to write this from the perspective of a 'normal' runner, with a job and a family, and just a few hours each week to give to it.

This book is specifically focused on marathon distance, as it is a different race to the 5k, 10k and half marathon in many ways. It is intended to take you through the steps to completing your first marathon, and for the more experienced athletes aiming to improve on their previous times.

I ran my first marathon in 2000 at the age of 27, completing London in a little below three and a half hours. It was hugely rewarding, but having completed this 'life-goal' I didn't consider running another event in the future. However, I came back to running after reluctantly giving up football in 2010, at the age of 37. This allowed me to focus purely on running and to improve significantly, and as a result enjoy my running far more and achieving the results that I wanted. My own personal goal was to see how fast I could go, to try to find my limit, as I approached the age of 40. The results surprised me, and continued to get gradually faster even after my 40th birthday.

To complete a marathon takes hard work and dedication, and if this is your first time you might feel nervous about being able to finish. However, if you follow a sensible program you will do it, and the sense of achievement from this can't be understated. Personally, I *loved* that I was now one of the few who had taken on this challenge, and completed it. If you are working towards your first marathon, you will already have a motivation, something driving you to this goal. Keep this in mind, for even if you never run again, the satisfaction of completing the 26.2 miles will stay with you for ever.

I've been lucky enough to travel around the world to run marathons – from my first race in London to Berlin, Amsterdam, Loch Ness, New York....and eventually back to the same local race in Newton Abbot in 2015. I finished in 2:44 with an overall race win. But the main point is that I didn't have to change my life, give up my job, risk divorce and so on....however, you have to be prepared to get up early, plan your training, and train more intelligently.

So, the first thing is to be clear and realistic about your objectives – do you want to complete one marathon, or several; do you want to go faster; are you aiming to clock up multiple events and join the 100 club; do you want to be the fastest dressed as a rhino / pantomime horse / hot dog; are you looking to get fit, and raise some money for charity? Apart from dressing up, all of these have been, and continue to be reasons for me.

Whether it's your first time, or you are working towards a faster time, if you have already committed to a race and have identified your aim, then you are a good deal of the way to your goal. This guide will provide you with some of the tools to get you there.

And remember, above all you should get out there and enjoy it.

15. Further Reading

Here is a very small selection of my favourite books and training programs, which I found helped me to improve my running, and to enjoy it more than ever.

In particular, for improving runners, Advanced Marathoning is highly informative.

- Advanced Marathoning – Pete Pfitzinger
- Hal Higdon's How to Train
- Performance Nutrition for Runners – Matt Fitzgerald

Printed in Great Britain
by Amazon